The Art of Convincing

Mastering Persuasion in the Digital Age

A brief introduction

You know that feeling when you read a message that just hits you and makes you want to take action right away?

Yeah, that's the power of persuasion! You'll learn all the techniques and tricks to trigger that same reaction in people with your words.

Don't think this is something from another world, no. None of that!
I'll show you how to use the right words, create impactful sentences and structure your messages in an irresistible way.

We want you to truly connect with your target audience. That's what will make the difference when it comes to convincing them to take action.

At the heart of this strategy is the power of persuasion techniques in writing.

A curious question...

Do you know what the most valuable skill in the world is?

Simple: the ability to sell.

Not just products and services,but ideas, concepts and beliefs.

Maybe you know it or not, but power goes to those who are persuasive, and that's true of every business in every country in the world.

It's important that you have a way to convince people (your boss, colleagues, clients, investors, etc.) that your ideas (and your work) are worthwhile.

I've identified a few key selling secrets over the years – a few tricks of the trade. And that's exactly what I'm going to share with you now – the foundations behind every great sales piece.

I call them THE THREE FUNDAMENTAL RULES OF SELLING and they are…

#1. People don't like the idea that they are being sold.

#2. People buy things for emotional reasons, not rational ones.

#3. Once they are bought, people need to excuse their emotional decisions with logic.

let's see **rule #1**: People don't like to be sold to them. At first, this doesn't make sense. Every year, trillions of dollars worth of goods and services are bought and sold... billions through the Post Office alone. Think about your friends. Many of them undoubtedly love shopping.

People like to buy things, but they don't like to be sold to them. Remember this. Whether you're writing a sales letter or trying to convince your friend to go to a concert, don't put the pressure on. Offer to give something. Don't force it, try it.

Let's say you want to get your friend to buy you a piece of chocolate cake. You wouldn't start by listing the 10 reasons why cake is good for him, would you? Of course not.

In real life, if you really wanted to get a friend to buy you a piece of cake, you'd probably start by describing how good the cake smells, how moist it is, how much frosting it has, and how it will melt in your mouth.
In other words, you would create a verbal image that triggers your cravings – your hunger, your desire for chocolate. You would tempt him by appealing to his emotions. You wouldn't bore him with reasons or force him.

Understand this first principle and you will have people eating out of your hand.

Rule #2 Hit where it hurts: People buy things for emotional reasons, not rational ones.

If people acted rationally, you couldn't sell chocolate cake.

There's no logical reason to eat it. It's not nutritious. Fattening. Kills metabolism. And it's expensive.

So why is chocolate cake a multi-million dollar industry?

Because it makes you feel good!

To be persuasive, you need to focus on your prospect's feelings and desires.

See seven important ones: fear, greed, vanity, lust, pride, envy and laziness.

Rule #3: As soon as the prospect has already bought emotionally, he needs to justify his irrational decision with rational reasons.

Now, you're ready to understand what copywriting is.

Copywriting

There is no way to talk about persuasion in the digital age without mentioning the famous Copywriting (or copy). This is one of the most essential elements of marketing.

It's the art and science of strategically delivering words (whether written or spoken) that get people to take action.

Nothing is more persuasive than someone who knows how to use words. If used well, they are capable of making someone make an instant decision. That's true Copywriting!

How did copywriting come about?

If you think Copywriting emerged these days, you're wrong. The first time the word "copy" was used was in the 19th century, in the year 1828.

Noah Webster, an American dictionary, defined copy as "an authorial creation to be imitated, both in writing and in print".

But the definition fell into disuse for years and only reappeared in 1870, when it started to describe professionals who wrote advertisements, differentiating themselves from traditional copywriters.

.

During the 19th century and throughout the 20th century, Copywriters' persuasive writing was mainly used in advertising copywriting.

The advancement of the internet and the growth of Digital

Marketing made Copywriting adopt a particular identity,

reformulated and distant from advertising.

The mess they made with advertising

Tell me something, what is advertising for you?

Is it something to be considered as work or as a work of art?

Is it clever slogans or amusing prose?

Is it work to be judged for an award or recognition?

I'm already advancing, it's none of the options above.

Advertising is a salesperson multiplied.
Just it.

And written advertising, or copywriting, is an art of selling whether on paper or digital.

The purpose of a copywriter's job is to sell. Full stop.

The sale is made by persuading with the written word, in the same way that a television commercial sells (*if done correctly of course*), coaxing with visual and audio effects.

As Claude Hopkins wrote in his timeless classic, Scientific Advertising:

"To understand advertising correctly, or even to learn the rudiments of it, one must start with correct perception.

Advertising is the art of selling. Its principles are the principles of the art of selling. Successes and failures in both lines are due to similar causes.

Thus, every advertising question must be answered by the seller's standards.

Let's emphasize this point. The sole purpose of advertising is to make sales.

It is not meant to give a general impression. It is not to put your name before people. It's not primarily made to help sellers.

Treat her like a salesperson.

It justifies itself.

Compare it with other sellers.

Record your costs and results.

Don't accept any excuses because good salespeople don't come up with them. And so you won't be far wrong.

Advertising is a salesperson multiplied. It can appeal to thousands while a salesperson only talks to one person. This is a corresponding cost.

Some people spend an average of $10 per word on an ad. Therefore, all ads must be a super seller.

A seller's mistake can cost little. An advertiser's mistake can cost a thousand times more. Therefore, be more cautious and more demanding. A mediocre salesperson can affect a small part of your business. Mediocre advertising affects your entire business.

These points are as true today as they were when they were written nearly a hundred years ago!

So the goal becomes: how can we make our advertising as effective as possible.

The answer is testing. Test again. And then test some more.

If ad "A" gets a two percent response rate, and ad "B" gets a three percent response rate, then we can deduce that ad "B" will continue to outperform ad "A".

But testing takes time, and can be expensive if not kept in check. So it's ideal to start with some proven ads, tried and tested ideas and work from there.

For example, if tests have shown over decades or more that targeted advertising significantly outperforms non-targeted advertising, then we can start with that assumption and work from there.

If we know from test results that making an ad that speaks directly to an individual works better than facing the masses, then it makes little sense to start testing with the assumption that it doesn't.

This is common sense.

So it stands to reason to know some basic rules or techniques about effective writing. Test results will always be the trump card, but it's best to have a starting point before testing.

So this starting point is the essence of this book.

The tips, expressed here, have generally been tested over time

and known to be effective.

But I can't stress enough that when using these techniques,

you should always test them out before launching a large,

expensive campaign.

Sometimes a small change here or there is all that is needed to

dramatically increase response rates.

And with that, let's move on........

Focus on them

And Not On You

When a prospect reads your ad, post, letter, etc., the only thing he'll be asking himself from the start is, "What's in it for me?"

And if your copy doesn't tell him anything, he'll end up in the trash faster than he can read the headline.

Many advertisers make this mistake. They focus on them as a company.

How long they've been open, who their biggest customers are, who's got ten years of research and millions of dollars in product development, blah, blah.

Indeed, these points are important.

But they must be expressed in a way that interests your prospect. Remember, once the ad is trashed, the sale is lost!

When writing your texts, it helps to think of them as a letter written to an old friend. In fact, I often picture a friend of mine who best fits my prospects' profile. What would I say to convince my friend to try my product?

How can I target my friend's objections and beliefs to help me?

When you're writing to a friend, you'll use the pronouns "I" and "you". When trying to convince your friend, you could say, "Hey, I know you think you've tried every gadget out there. But you should know that..."

And this goes beyond just writing in the second person. That is, treat your prospects as "you" in your texts. The fact is, there are many successful ads that aren't written in the second person.

Some are written in first person perspective where the writer uses "I". Other times, the third person is used, such as "she", "he", and "they".

And even if you write in the second person, it doesn't necessarily mean your copy is about them.

For example:

"Being a real estate agent, you can take solace in the fact that I have sold over 10,000 homes and have mastered the tricks of the trade."

Although you are writing in the second person, you are still focusing on yourself.

So how can you focus on them?

Glad you asked.

One way is...

Stages of Consumer Awareness

Level of awareness here basically means whether the prospect is aware of your product or is aware that there is a solution to their problem.

Knowing exactly where it is will determine the type of content you write.

Figuring this out can increase conversions 2X or more.

Legendary copywriter Gene Schwartz gave the following rule:

If the potential customer is already familiar with the product and knows it can help them, the headline should start with the product.
If your avatar doesn't know your product but has a desire, you lead with that desire.

Finally, if the prospect doesn't really know what they need but just has a general problem, you start with the problem and write copy to make the prospect realize they need your solution.

Those are the basics. Gene laid out 5 levels of customer awareness that explain this concept in more detail, and that's what I'm going to get into now.

So your 5 levels of customer awareness are:

Level 1 - is the most attentive customer - this person knows what he wants, he trusts you, and when you offer him something new, there is a good chance that he will buy it. These customers are what every marketer wants. For example, think of brands that have a following like Nike and Apple. The consumer knows the brand and wants the product, there is no effort at the time of sale.

Level 2 - product aware. These people don't trust you yet - they know you're selling them something they want, but they're not sure it's right for them. Since they still don't trust you, they read reviews, look at testimonials, and try to determine if your product can do what you say it can. With prospects like these, the goal of your copy should be to immediately reassure them. These first two categories, by the way, are the easiest to make sales. As your avatar becomes less aware, you have a tougher job ahead of you.

Alright, the next level of customer awareness is solution awareness.

Level 3 - These are people who have a problem, they know there is a solution to it, but they don't know your product and the results they can get with it. With prospects like these, you want them to know that you understand their desires and that your product will help them get there.

As we move further into awareness, we start to reach those prospects who can really help your business grow.

So the next type of customer awareness is problem awareness.

Level 4 - This is someone who is worried – he feels he has a problem, but he doesn't know there is a solution to it. With this type of customer, you want your lead to show them that you understand their frustration and anxiety.

Finally, there is the completely unaware client.

Level 5 - These people are a hard sell to them. They don't realize they have a problem, they don't know anything about your brand, and they don't even know there's a solution to what they're experiencing. With this type of person, you will have to come up with a powerful and extremely irresistible offer. You need to present your offer as if it were a drawing, where people can see all the details, even see the colors, smell, taste and texture of what you are offering.

Understanding and adapting to different levels of consumer awareness is critical to building an effective marketing strategy.

By adjusting your message, approach and tactics according to the stage the consumer is in, you can increase the chances of engagement, conversion and loyalty.

By taking into account the 5 levels of consumer awareness, you will be better prepared to meet your target audience's needs, establish a meaningful connection, and build lasting relationships.

Deepen your knowledge of consumer behavior, research and test your strategies and always be willing to adapt to market changes and demands. That way, you'll be well on your way to success in your marketing and sales efforts.

Also, remember that consumers can transition between different levels of consciousness over time.

They can start at the level of unconsciousness and, through information and interactions, progress to the next stages.

Therefore, it is essential to keep a close eye on the behavior of your target audience, so that you can adjust your strategy as needed.

Another important point to consider is the importance of clear and consistent communication at each stage of consciousness.

Whether through educational content, storytelling, testimonials or product demonstrations, it is essential to convey your message effectively and relevantly.

By doing this, you will be nurturing consumer trust and creating an emotional connection with your brand.

How to enhance the benefits

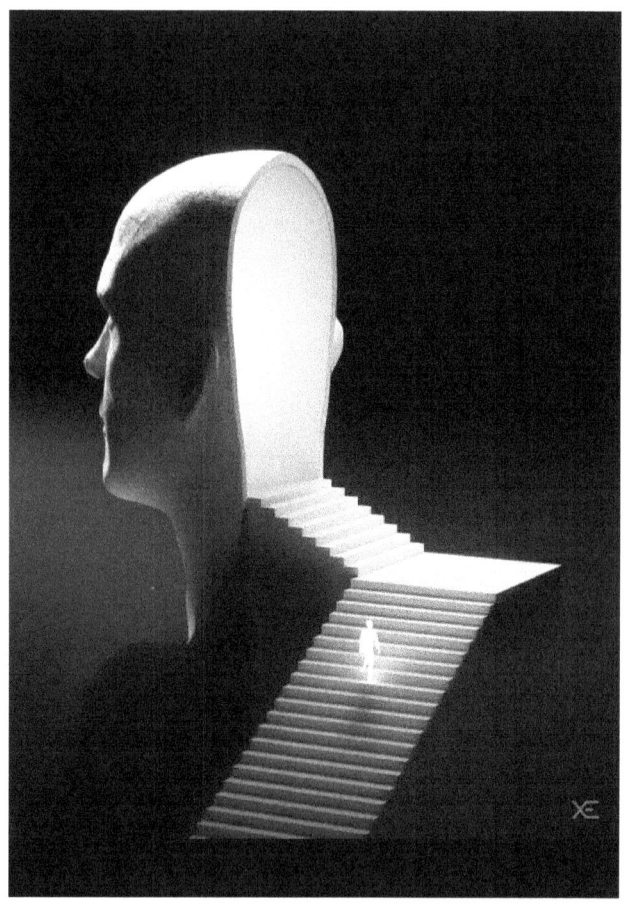

And the what are the features?

They are descriptions of the qualities that a product has.

• The XYZ car does 55 kilometers per liter in the city

• Frame is made of durable, lightweight steel.

• Our glue is protected by a patent.

• This database has an internal data search system.

But what are the benefits?

Well, they are what the results mean to your prospects.

• You'll save money on gas and reduce environmental pollutants when you use our high-performance energy-saving hybrid car. Plus, you'll feel the extra power when you're passing other cars, courtesy of the efficient electric motor, which they don't have!

• Lightweight durable alloy steel frame means you'll be able to take it with ease, and use it in places other ladders can't go, while supporting up to 800 pounds. No back pain when dragging a heavy ladder. And as it will last 150 years, you'll never need to buy another ladder again!

• Patented glue ensures you can use it on wood, plastic, ceramics, metal, glass and tile... no messy cleanups and no re-gluing - guaranteed!

• You can instantly get the "big picture" hidden in your dice, and pull out the most arcane stats whenever you want.

Watch your business go "180" quickly as you instantly know what's failing!

It's all done with our data search system which is so easy to use, my twelve year old son used it successfully as soon as he started using it.

I created these examples, but I think you understand what I mean.

NOTE: You are not writing to impress your Portuguese teacher or win an award.

The only prize you want to win is that your text sells and beats your previous best ad, while having some freedom in grammar, punctuation and sentence structure. You want it to be read and acted upon, not read and admired!

But back to the benefits…

If you were selling an expensive watch, wouldn't you tell your reader that the watch case is 5 inches in diameter and the strap is made of leather.

You should show him how the extra-large display will tell you the time at a glance. Oh yeah!

He doesn't want to have to go looking for the time on the clock and look foolish in front of everyone around him trying to read this magnificent clock.

And how about the way he projects success and charisma when he wears the gold watch with its beautiful custom crafted leather strap?

How irresistible his sweetheart will find him when he's all dressed up to go out, wearing his watch. Or how the status and beauty of the watch will appeal to the ladies.

By the way, did you notice that I stressed that seeing well is a benefit?

Does that seem like a silly benefit?

Not if you're selling to baby boomers who suffer from poor eyesight.

They probably hate it when someone they're trying to impress sees them squint and try to read something.

It's all about your inner desires, that's what you need to find out. And that even they might not even know.

That is…until you show them a better way.

The point here is to address the benefits of the product, not its features. And when you do that, you're focusing on your reader and their interests, their desires.

The trick is to highlight the specific benefits that push your reader's emotional buttons.

How do you do it?

I'll show!

The Big Idea and the Rule of One

Whenever the subject is copywriting, the concept of the "Big Idea" comes to the fore. David Ogilvy talks about him and several other authors like Michael Masterson and John Forde, authors of the book Great Leads, too.

The concept is quite simple, but a lot of people get it wrong.

Basically, the Big Idea, or Rule of One, proposes that your text focus on just one action, one promise, one idea that must be objective and without "accessories".

I'll put some examples here for you to compare and understand the difference of the Big Idea.

Examples without the Big Idea:

Lists (161 New Ways to Win a Man's Heart…);

Generic Plurals (The Crimes We Commit Against Our Stomachs)

Examples with the Big Idea:

Specific (The Secret to Getting People to Like You);

Directed (To Men Who Want To Quit One Day);

Impact (Is a Child's Life Worth $1 to You?).

Despite being somewhat appealing examples (extracted from the book Great Leads), the difference between the Great Idea in these titles is clear, isn't it?

Can you tell what the focal point of the first two examples is? It's hard to say, as they are quite comprehensive and unfocused.

However, examples using the Big Idea framework are much more focused.

Therefore, we can safely say about the subject that they introduce, even if we have no knowledge about the product to which they are linked.

So, be very clear on what your Big Idea is. To do this, you must work with the following structure:

A good idea: show the benefits or advantages of the product/solution you are selling;

a core emotion: create a connection with the reader, provoking engagement from emotional reinforcement so that the rational continues to progress in the text;

a captivating story: Reinforces the core emotion. It is often a case, an episode or it brings data and numbers that prove your offer (product/service);

A unique and desirable benefit: consolidates the advantage (benefit) that your product or service offers to the reader;

An inevitable answer: point out the path that must be followed for your reader to reach the benefit you are talking about.

This is all so that we can support the title from an introduction (called, in this context, a lead) that must use the correct technique, depending on the reader's level of awareness.

This technique can be a story, a prediction, a statement, a promise, etc.).

Regardless of which one you use, it's important that your single Big Idea is backed up by an equally unique emotion, in order to direct the reader to the desired action.

Pressing Emotional Buttons

Here is where research really pays off. Because, to press the buttons, you first need to know what they are.

Watch this story, and you'll understand what I mean: once upon a time, a young man walked into a certain Chevrolet dealership to see a Chevy Camaro.

He had money, and he was ready to make a buying decision. But he couldn't decide whether he wanted to buy the Camaro or the Ford Mustang on his way to the Ford dealership.

A salesman approached him and soon discovered the man's dilemma.

"Tell me what you like best about the Camaro," the salesman said.

"It's a fast car. I like its speed."

After some discussion, the salesman learned that the man had started dating a college cheerleader.

So what did the seller do?

Simple. He changed his pitch and pushed emotional buttons that way, because he knew it would help drive the sale.

He told the man that his new girlfriend would be impressed when he got home in this car!

He put the mental image in the man's mind that he and his girlfriend were traveling to the beach in the Camaro.

And how jealous all his friends would be when they saw him driving around with a nice girl in a nice car.

And suddenly the man had the vision. He got it. And the seller saw this and worked on this point. And before you know it, the man writes a nice check to the Chevrolet dealership!

The salesman found the emotional buttons and pushed them like never before until the man realized he wanted the Camaro more than he wanted his money.

I know what you're thinking... the man said he liked the car because it was fast, didn't he?
Yes that was it. But subconsciously, what he really wanted was a car that would impress his girlfriend, his friends, and in his mind make them like him even more! In his mind, he equates speed with emotion.

Not because he wanted an endless amount of speeding tickets, but because he thought the thrill would make him more attractive, and more enjoyable.

Perhaps the man did not even realize this fact. But the seller noticed. And he knew what emotional buttons he had to press to get the sale.

Now, why does research pay off?

Well, a good salesperson knows how to ask the questions that will tell you which buttons to press quickly. When you're writing sales copy, you don't have that luxury.
Therefore, for this very reason, it is very important to know your customers' wants, needs and desires in advance.

If you haven't done your homework, your prospect will decide he'd rather keep his money than buy your product.

Remember, copywriting is the paper or digital seller!

It's been said many times: People don't like to be sold.

But they like to shop.

And they buy first and foremost based on emotion.

Then they justify their decision with logic, even after they've already been emotionally sold. So be sure to back up your emotional speech with logic to nurture justification at the end.

And while we're on the subject, let's talk a little about sales page hype. Many "conservative" marketers have decided that they don't like hype, because they consider hype to be "old style", they already have, and they think customers won't fall for it, it's no longer credible.

What they must understand is that it's not the exaggerations themselves that don't sell well.

Some less experienced copywriters often try to compensate for their lack of research or not fully understanding their target market or their own product by adding tons of adjectives, adverbs and exclamation points and lots of bold.

Really! If you do your job, this is not necessary.

That's not to say that some adverbs or adjectives don't have their place... only if they're used in moderation, and only if they advance the sale.

I think you would agree that backing up your texts with evidence and credibility will go much further in convincing your potential customers than using "power words" alone.

I say power words because there are certain adjectives and adverbs that have been proven to make a difference when they are included.

This in itself is not an exaggeration. But repeated too many times, they become less effective.

Which brings us to our next tip...

There will always be objections

Objections are psychological barriers that arise in the minds of consumers, generating resistance to the offers presented.

Understanding objections and being able to overcome them is essential to increasing the conversion rate and driving the success of marketing campaigns.

The Nature of Objections

It is important to recognize that objections are a natural defensive response from consumers. In an increasingly saturated market with a large volume of information, consumers are increasingly cautious in relation to their purchase decisions.

Purchasing a product or service is seen as an investment, and it is natural for people to have doubts and concerns before committing to it.

Identifying the Objections

To get around objections, it is essential to identify them clearly and precisely.

By analyzing interactions with your target audience, whether through surveys, feedback or data analysis, it is possible to identify the main concerns and resistance that consumers have in relation to your offers. This allows you to understand the underlying reason behind these objections and find effective ways to overcome them.

Addressing the Objections

When addressing objections, it is crucial to convey confidence and provide relevant information that allays the public's concerns.

Objection breaking involves providing strong, persuasive arguments that demonstrate the value and benefits of your offering, while respecting consumers' legitimate concerns.

An effective strategy for overcoming objections is to anticipate them. When developing your marketing content, whether in ads, emails or sales pages, you can anticipate the most common objections and proactively address them. This involves providing information that counters concerns before they even arise in consumers' minds.

When responding to objections, it is important to use an empathetic and personalized approach.

Show that you understand your target audience's concerns and provide clear, relevant information that dispels them.

Use real examples, testimonials from satisfied customers, and case studies to demonstrate how your offering overcomes objections and meets consumers' needs.

Another effective strategy is to offer guarantees and extra benefits that reduce the risk perceived by the consumer.

Offering a satisfaction guarantee, a free trial period or an exclusive bonus can help reassure consumers and encourage them to overcome their objections and take the desired action.

Furthermore, creating a sense of urgency can also be effective in breaking down objections. By offering limited-time promotions or highlighting limited product or service availability, you create a sense of urgency that motivates consumers to take action. This feeling of scarcity can be a determining factor in overcoming objections, as consumers fear losing the opportunity if they don't act immediately.

It is critical to highlight the competitive differentiators of your product or service when addressing objections. Show how it stands out from the competition and offers unique solutions to your target audience's problems and needs. By highlighting the strengths of your offering, you're providing clear reasons for consumers to overcome their objections and choose your brand.

Transparency is key in breaking objections. Be honest about your offering's limitations or challenges, but also highlight the benefits and solutions it provides. Honesty builds trust and credibility, key elements to overcoming consumer objections.

It is important to emphasize that objection breaking is not about manipulation or aggressive persuasion. The aim is to provide relevant information, answer legitimate questions and help consumers make informed decisions. The focus should be on building long-term relationships and providing value to customers, rather than just chasing a quick sale.

By identifying the most common objections, anticipating them, and addressing them empathetically and persuasively, you'll be well on your way to winning your target audience's trust and motivating them to take action.

Finally, always be willing to listen to consumer feedback and adapt your strategies according to their needs and concerns. Constantly perfecting your objection-breaking techniques will help you stand out in the marketplace, gain consumer trust, and achieve positive, lasting results.

Incorporating Evidence and Credibility

When your prospect reads your ad, you want to make sure he believes all the claims you make about your product or service. Because if there's any doubt in his mind, he won't bite, no matter how sweet the deal is.

In fact, the "too good to be true" mentality will practically guarantee having a lost sale... even if it's all true.

So what can you do to increase perceived credibility?

Because after all, it's the perception you need to sort out.

But of course you should also make sure your text is accurate and truthful.

Here are some tried and true methods that will help:

• If you're dealing with your existing customers who already know you deliver what you promise, emphasize that trust. Don't let them figure it out. Make them stop, nod their heads yes, and say, "Yes. ABC Company has never done me wrong before. I can trust them."

• Include testimonials from satisfied customers. Don't forget to put the full name and place where possible.
Remember, "José" is much less convincing than "Armando Soares, Rio De Janeiro, Brazil." You can also include a customer photo and/or a professional title, which is even better. It doesn't matter if your testimonials aren't from someone famous or that your prospect doesn't know these people personally.

If you have sufficiently compelling testimonials, and they are credible, you are doing a much better job than not including them.

• Spice up your texts with facts and research findings to support your claims. Be sure of all sources of information, even if the fact is common knowledge, as a neutral source does not lend much credibility.

• In direct offer letters or certain advertisements where the texts are in the form of a letter from a specific individual, it helps to include a photo of that person.

But unlike "traditional" real estate industry letters and other similar advertisements, I would place the photo at the end of the letter, near your signature, or in the middle of the copy, rather than at the top because it will detract from your headline.

And... if your sales letter is from a specific individual, be sure to include their credentials establishing them as an expert in their field (related to your product or service, of course).

• If applicable, cite any third-party awards or reviews that the third-party product or service has received.

• If you've sold a lot of products, tell them. It's the old adage "10 million people can't be wrong" (those 10 million could be wrong, but your prospect will probably side with you on this one).

• Include a return policy and make it clear! It's just good business policy. Often, offering a double money-back guarantee for certain products will result in higher profits.

Yes, you'll get more refunds, but if you sell three times as much product as before, and only have to refund twice as much as before, it might be worth it, depending on your offer and return on investment.

Crunch the numbers and see what makes sense. Most importantly, test! Make them think, "Wow, they wouldn't be so generous with returns if it's not what they're promising about their product!"

• If you can add a celebrity endorsement, it helps establish credibility. Wow, if Pele recommends your product and backs up what you promise, it must be true! .

• When it makes sense, use third-party testimonials. What are third-party testimonials? Here are some examples of some websites I wrote when I didn't have many customer testimonials yet.

"Spyware, without any doubt, has seen an exponential increase in the last six months."
- Alfred Huger, Director of Engineering, Symantec Security Response (maker of Norton's security software)

"Just click on a banner and you can install spyware."
- Dave Methvin, Chief Technology Officer, PC Pitstop

One deployment method is to "fool users into consenting to download software they think they absolutely need"
- Paul Bryan, Director of Security and Technology Unit, Microsoft.

Did you see what I did?

I used quotes from experts in their respective fields and turned them around for my purposes.
But be sure to get their consent or permission from the copyright holder, if there is any need to use copyrighted materials ask about their source.

Note that I also pressed an emotional button: fear.
It has been proven that people generally do more to avoid pain than to gain pleasure.

So why not use this tidbit of information to your advantage?

• Reveal a flaw in your product. This helps alleviate the "too good to be true" syndrome.

Reveal a glitch that isn't really a glitch. Or reveal a flaw that is minor, just to show that you are being open about your product's shortcomings.

example:

"You're probably thinking right now that this tennis racket is a miracle - and it is. But I have to tell you that it has a small defect.

My racket takes about 2 weeks to get used to.

In fact, once you start using it, your game will actually go downhill. But if you continue to use it, you will see a tremendous improvement in your serves, net play, and so on.

There's a tendency to think, with all the ads we're bombarded with these days, that each advertiser is always showing only what's best. And I think that line of reasoning is open.

But isn't it refreshing when someone stands out from the crowd and is honest? In other words, the reader will subconsciously start to believe that you are revealing all the flaws.

• Use "Praise Notes" These brief notes are from a person in authority. Not necessarily from a celebrity, although that can also add credibility.

A person of authority is someone recognized in their field (which is related to your product) and who is qualified to speak. Praised notes can be distributed as inserts, on a separate page, or even as part of the text. As always, test!

• If you are limiting the offer with a deadline that ends by a certain date, make sure the deadline is real and does not change. Deadlines that change every day reduce credibility.

The prospect will be suspicious "if the deadline keeps changing, he's not telling the truth... I wonder what else he's not telling the truth about".

• Avoid "overkill". Unfounded that I discussed in my previous tip. Enough said.

The Unique Value Proposition

The PUV is often one of the most often misunderstood elements of a good sales letter.

It's what separates your product or service from your competitors. Let's take a quick look at some unique selling propositions for a product;

1) Lowest Price - If you have your business in the low-price area, flaunt it. Wal-Mart has made this PUV famous lately, but it's not new to them.

Selling cheaper has been around for as long as capitalism has. I don't like price wars, because someone can come along and sell cheaper.

So it's time for a new strategy.

2) Superior Quality- If it outperforms your competitor's product or is made with high quality materials, it's a good bet that you use this fact to your advantage.

For example, compare your product to your competitors. From superior packaging to healthy ingredients, the quality is evident. It might cost a little more than your competitor, but for your market, it sells.

3) Service - If you offer superior service over your competition, people will buy from you. This is especially true in certain markets that are very service related: long distance, Internet service providers, cable television, etc.

4) Exclusive Rights – My favorite! If you can legitimately claim that your product is protected by a patent or copyright, licensing agreement, etc., then you have an exclusive right as a winner. If you have a patent, even the President has to buy it from you.

Okay, isn't your product or service different from your competitor's? I disagree, because there are always differences. The trick is to turn them to your positive advantage. So what can we do about this scenario?

One way is to present something your company has developed internally that no other company does.

Look, there's a reason why computer store "A" offers to beat its competitors' prices for the same product at X.

If you look closely, the two packages are never exactly the same. Company "B" offers a free scanner, while Company "A" offers a printer. Or some other difference. They are comparing apples to oranges.

So unless you find a company with the exact same package (you won't..they studied that) you won't be able to win the promotion.

But what if you actually have the same device for sale as the guy across the street?

Unless your prospect knows the inner workings of both your and your competitor's product, including the manufacturing process, customer service, and everything in between, then you have the potential to be given license for a little creativity. But you must be true.

For example, if I tell my readers that my product is steam bathed to ensure purity and cleanliness (like the cans and bottles in most brewing processes), it doesn't matter that Joe's beer across the street does the same. thing.

The fact that John does not announce this fact makes it hisunique product in the eyes of your prospect.

Want more PUV examples?

• We are the only car repair shop that will buy your car if you are not 100 percent satisfied with our work.
• Delivered in 30 minutes or on us!
• No furniture company will pay for your shipping.
• Our recipe is so secret that only three people in the world know it!

As with most ways to increase response, research is key with your PUV. Sometimes your PUV is obvious, for example when you have a patent. Other times you must do a little research work to figure it out (or shape it for your target market).

This is where a little persistence really pays off.

Let me give you an example to illustrate what I mean: Suppose your company sells puffs for children. So you, being the wise marketer that you are, decide to sell the puffs to prospects before writing your sales copy.

After you've given about twenty different sales pitches for your product, you find that 75 percent of the people you spoke to asked if the puffs would eventually leak.

Since puffs are for children, it only stands to reason that parents would be concerned about their youngsters jumping on them, rolling on them, and doing every possible thing to break the seam and deflate the puff.

So when you write your copy, you make sure you address this question: "You can be sure that our super-strong poufs are triple-stitched so leak-proof performance is guaranteed. No other company will do this." warranty on your puffs!

THE UNIQUE MECHANISM

This is the most important point of your marketing and perhaps your life. If you master it, chances are you'll never have to worry about the competition again.

Have you ever stopped to think about how many products similar to yours exist? How many people with skills similar to yours are walking around?

What will be the secret, then, for a few people and products to stand out? The answer is: the unique mechanism.

Yes, it's a mechanism. It's not a point, it's not a sentence, but an operating scheme capable of bringing the solution to the other, in the simplest, most effective and different way than anything that has ever been seen.

To exemplify, let's look at something very common... frying pans.

But what do frying pans have to do with my business? ALL!

You can find frying pans for R$40.00. However, many people have already been tempted to buy the Polishop frying pan (if they haven't already)... the one that costs more than R$200.00 and you see it on TV. If you haven't seen it yet, I recommend you see it.

Oh, and no, it doesn't stand out because it's on TV. After all, you ignore hundreds of other commercials...

This is just one clear example. But every big business I've seen to date has a unique mechanism for their products and services, even if you don't see it as clearly as Polishop does. All the people who get the best jobs in companies sell themselves with a unique mechanism.

Therefore, if you want to stand out to escape the fight over prices and awaken the desire of others, answer 3 questions:

- Why does my product/service solve people's problems?

- How does my product/service lead people to the success they see?

- What differentiates my product / service from everything that exists?

Believe me, it works from markets with little competition to the most disputed ones. By the way, it is totally ethical, if you work only with the truth.

I myself have already created dozens of mechanisms for the weight loss sector, for example, which today is an extremely competitive sector, in addition to being very delicate because we are talking about health.

The key to the mechanism is KNOWING that you are UNIQUE (we all are, however much some would try to say that we are replaceable) and highlighting your strengths.

HEADLINE

If you're going to make a single change to increase your response rate, focus on your headline (*you have one, don't you?*).

Why? Because there will be five times more people reading your title than your text. Quite simply, a headline...is an ad for your ad.

People won't stop their busy lives to read your text unless you give them a good reason to do so.

Thus, a good title promises some news and a benefit.

Maybe you're thinking, "What's with the news?"

Think back to the last time you "browsed" through your local newspaper.

You skimmed through the articles one by one, and occasionally an ad might have grabbed your attention. What ads were most likely to get your attention?

The ones that looked like an article, of course.

Those with a title that promises news.

Those with typefaces that closely resembled the typefaces used in articles.

The ones that were placed where the articles were placed (as opposed to being placed on a page full of ads, for example).

And those with the most compelling headlines that convince you they're worth a few minutes to read the text.

The title is therefore powerful and important.

I've seen many ads over the years that don't even have a headline. And that's silly. It's the equivalent of wasting good money spent on advertising.

Why? Because your response can increase dramatically, not by adding a title, but by making that title almost irresistible to your target audience.

And those last three words are important. "Your target audience".

For example. Take a look at the following title:

Announcing... New State-of-the-Art Gloves That Protect Against Hazardous Waste.

News, and a benefit

Does the title appeal to everyone?

No, and you don't care at all.

But for people who deal with hazardous waste, they will definitely be glad to know about this little gem.

This is your target audience, and it's your job to get them to read your ad. Your title is the way to do this.

Okay, now where do you find the big headlines?

You look at other successful ads (especially direct response) that have stood the test of time. You look at the regularly used advertisements in magazines and other publications. How do you know they are good?

Because if they didn't do their job, the advertiser wouldn't keep putting them up over and over again.

You sign up for the list of great direct response companies and save the emails.

Do you read magazines about celebrities?

Celebrity magazines have some of the best headlines.

Pick up a recent issue and you'll see what I mean. Okay, now how can you adapt some of these headlines for your own service or product?

The appearance of your title is also very important. Make sure the type used is bold and large, and different from the type used in the text. Generally, longer titles tend to outperform shorter ones, even when targeting more "conservative" prospects.

This way you use other people's hit titles, but adapt them for your own product or service. Never copy a title (or any other piece of writing) word for word. Copywriters and advertising agencies are notorious for prosecuting plagiarism. And with every right.

When More You Say,

More You Will Sell

The debate about using long textversus Short texts don't seem to end.

It's usually a newcomer to the copywriting world who seems to think long texts are boring. They say "I would never read so many texts".

The fact is, all things being equal, long copy will always outperform short copy, and when I say long copy, I don't mean long, boring copy, or long, untargeted copy.

The person who says he would never read all of the text is making a huge mistake in copywriting: he is following his gut reaction instead of relying on test results. She is thinking that he himself is the prospect. And she is not. We are never our own prospects.

There have been many studies and tests on long texts versus short texts. And the winner is always long text. But I'm talking about long, relevant text rather than boring, untargeted long text.

Some significant research has found that readings tend to drop dramatically after 300 words, but not again until around 3,000 words.

If I'm selling an expensive set of golf clubs and I send my long text to a person who plays golf occasionally or has always wanted to try golf, I'm sending my sales pitch to the wrong prospect.

Not an effective target. And so, if a person who receives my long text doesn't read past 300 words, they're not eligible for my offer.

It wouldn't matter if they read to word 100 or 10,000. They wouldn't make the purchase either way.

However, if I send my text to an avid golfer, who has recently purchased other expensive golf products through the mail, painting an irresistible offer, telling him how his game will improve in 10 strokes, he probably will. read every word. And if I've targeted my message correctly, he'll buy.

Remember, if your prospect is 3000 kilometers away, it's not easy for him to ask a question. If you want to be successful, you must anticipate and answer all their questions and overcome all objections in your text.

And make sure you don't throw everything you can think of into the text. You only need to include as much information as you need to make the sale... and not another word.

If it takes 10 pages of text, so be it. If it takes a 16-page megalog, fine. But if in tests 10 pages sell better than the 16 pages megalog, then go with the winner.

Does that mean every prospect must read every word of your copy before he or she orders your product? Of course.

Some will read every word and then go back and reread it again.

Some will read the title and keep going, skipping most of the body and landing at the end. Some will scan the entire body, then go back and read it. All of those prospects could end up buying the offer, but they could have all different reading styles.

And that brings us to the next tip.

Write Scannably

I just love formatsscannable, see the example below:

Suddenly

If I tell you a story

in this format

No accurate information

But with a high emotional charge...

maybe you'll be moved

Why is the story so vague?

What could have happened to you!

But that

hand passes

from a text

Made to manipulate your emotions

saying a lot

Without saying anything.

Your layout is very important in sales text, because you want your text to look inviting, refreshing to the eyes. In short, you want your prospect to stop what they're doing and read your copy.

If he sees text with small margins, no indentations, no breaks in the text, no white space, and no subheadings...

If he sees a page, with words packed tightly together, do you think he'll be tempted to read it?

If you have white space with wide, generous margins, short sentences, short paragraphs, subheadings, and an italicized or underlined word here and there for emphasis, he will certainly be interested in reading.

When reading your copy, some prospects will start at the beginning and read it word for word. Some will read the headline and perhaps the subheading, then read the "PS" at the end of the text and see whose text it is from, and then start at the beginning.

Some people will scan the text, looking at the various subheadings strategically placed by you throughout your text, then deciding if it's worth their time to read the whole thing. Some may never read the entire text but buy anyway.

You must write to all of them. Long, interesting, and engaging text for the detail-oriented reader, and short paragraphs and sentences, white space, and subheadings for jumpers.

Subheadings are the smaller headings scattered throughout the text.

When you are in the process of creating a title, some of the titles that are not good enough will be good as subtitles. A subheadline forces your prospect to keep reading, captivating them from the beginning to the end of your entire copy.

The Framework That Can Save You From Writer's Block

There is a well-known structure to successful sales pages, described by the acronym AIDA.

AIDA stands for:

• Attention

• Interest

• Desire

• Action

First, you capture your prospect's attention. This is done with your title. If the ad fails to capture your prospect's attention, it fails completely. Your prospect doesn't read your star copy, and they don't order your product or service.

Then you build strong interest in your prospect. You want him to keep reading because if he keeps reading he might buy.

Next, you channel a wish. Having a target audience for this is key because you're not trying to create a craving in someone who doesn't. You want to capitalize on an existing desire that your prospect may or may not know he already has. And you want your prospect to want the experience your product or service offers.

Finally, you present a call to action. You want him to pick up the phone, return the reply letter, watch the sales presentation, order your product, or whatever.

You need to ask for the sale (or an answer, if that's the goal). You don't want to beat around the bush at this point. If your letter and AIDA structure is solid and compelling, this is where you lay out the terms of your offer and want the prospect to act now.

Much has been written about copywriting the AIDA formula. And I would like to add one more letter to the acronym: S for Satisfy
In the end, after the sale is made, you want to satisfy your prospect, who is now a customer.

You have to deliver exactly what you promised (or even more), on the deadlines you promised, in the way you promised.

In short, you want to give him every reason in the world to trust you the next time you offer him a new offer.

And of course you want him not to return the product to you (although if he does, you should enforce your return policy as promised).

Either way, you want your customers to be happy. They will make you a lot more money in the long run.

Learn how to Raise an Urgency

When you limit the supply of a product or service in some way (i.e. limited sale), basic economics dictate that demand will increase.

In other words, people generally respond better to an offer if they believe the offer is about to become unavailable or restricted in some way.

And, of course, the opposite is also true. If a prospect knows the product will be available whenever he needs it, there's no need to act now.

And when your ad is pushed aside by your prospect, the chances of closing the sale are greatly reduced.

So your job is to get your customers to buy, and buy now. Using scarcity to sell is a great way to accomplish this.

There are basically three types of limitations:

1 - Limit the quantity

2 - Limit the time

3 - Limit to offer

In the first method, limiting quantity, you are presenting a fixed number of products available for sale. When they're gone, it's over.

Some good ways to limit the amount include:

• Only have a certain amount of units made

• The sale of old stock to make room for new

• Limited number of items with cosmetic defect

• Only a number of products will be sold so as not to saturate the market.

• Etc.

In the second method, limiting time, the deadline is added to the offer. It should be a realistic deadline, not one that changes all the time (especially on a site, where the deadline seems to be close to midnight... when you come back the next day, the deadline has mysteriously changed to that day). Changing deadlines diminish your credibility.

This approach works well when the offer, or the price will change, or the product/service will become unavailable after the end date.

The third method, limiting the offer, is accomplished by limiting other parts of the offer, such as the guarantee, bonuses or prizes, pricing and so on.

When using the limited sale, you must be sure to comply with the restrictions. If you say you only have 500 items to sell, then don't sell 501. If you say your offer will expire at the end of the month, make sure it does.

Otherwise, your credibility will go down. Prospects will remember the next time you throw another offer into their hands.

Another important thing you should do is explain why the offer is being restricted. Don't just say that the price will go up in three weeks, but explain why it will go up.

Here are some examples of limited sales:

"Unfortunately, I can only handle a limited number of clients. Once my time is full, I will be unable to take on any other business.

So if you are serious about enhancing your investment strategies and creating more wealth than ever before, you should contact me ASAP. "

"Remember: you must act by [date] midnight in order to get my 2 bonuses.

These bonuses were offered by [third-party company], and we have no control over their availability after this period. "

We only have 750 of these items from our supplier. Once they run out, we won't be able to get more until next year.

And even then we cannot guarantee that the price will remain the same. In fact, because of increasing demand, the price is very likely to double or triple by then! "

Remember what I said earlier, people buy based on emotions, and then make their buying decision with logic. Well, using the limited sale, the restriction becomes part of the buy and buy now logic.

Whether you realize it or not, you now know more about

creating effective advertising than most of your competitors.

Want to prove it?

Ask them about any of the ideas we discussed. In response, you will likely get wrong answers and blank stares.

That's because most of your competitors are too busy running their businesses to stop and

learn how to make them more successful. I congratulate you for doing so. In fact, the little-known tips, tricks, techniques, and principles I've shared

with you here are the same as a marketing consultant

or advertising agency would use if you hired them for a lot of money. There's no reason why you can't use them and reap the best rewards.

Conclusion

Good copywriting is made, not born.

It's derived from proven test results designed to do one thing and do it well: Sell.

Effective advertising is not always "grammatically correct".

She uses short sentences and snippets.

Convince them to buy, and buy now. Full stop.

Talk about benefits, not features. Sell emotion in the ad and reinforce the decision to buy with logic.

Paint a compelling picture and come up with an irresistible offer that compels your prospect to take action and take action now! And if it doesn't, then you don't have any interest in the ad.

Effective persuasion is like your top salesperson who keeps breaking records for all of his sales for the year, multiplied by thousands or millions!

Imagine if that salesperson, the one with proven results, could be multiplied as many times as you'd like.

That's effective marketing!

This is the proven type of marketing you need to use.

I wish you great results going forward.